I0490708

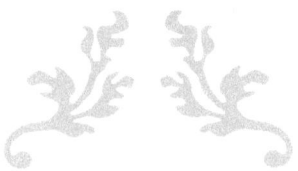

HOW TO GET 360 WAVES

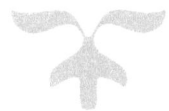

AMAZON CORPORATE
505 west Garret st, Box 151 Calvert,Tx77837

How TO Get 360 waves

Tyrone* 360 Wave Deep Pizza* Huffman

Waves R
Us

ACKNOWLEDGMENTS

To my family friends and my kids and grand children and the almighty God

My mother and brother, step daughters, and my kids mothers couldn't do it with out you all.

Introduction

The miracle of believing and taking your time out to be your best a lot of people like braids and they were low hair cuts, and we call that a table fade or the college cut, but when you are rocking them waves you are making your hair look healthy and shiny and very compatible, to teach others and given grooming tips. 360 waves is also part of and African American culture, because it show

HOW TO GET 360 WAVES

we as black man, how we love our hair and this book will show that, people spend tunes of money on products to begin the 360 wave process. But all it takes is time and knowing which way to brush. So in this book I will show my 360 waves methods on how to get 360 waves the right way, and I will speak on very important topics .

Because we all have the power to be a wave king and also to be your own barber, so let us learn on how to get them 360 waves popping. And me 360 waves deep pizza will show you how and share powerful secrets and why 360 waves is important to the black community and culture.

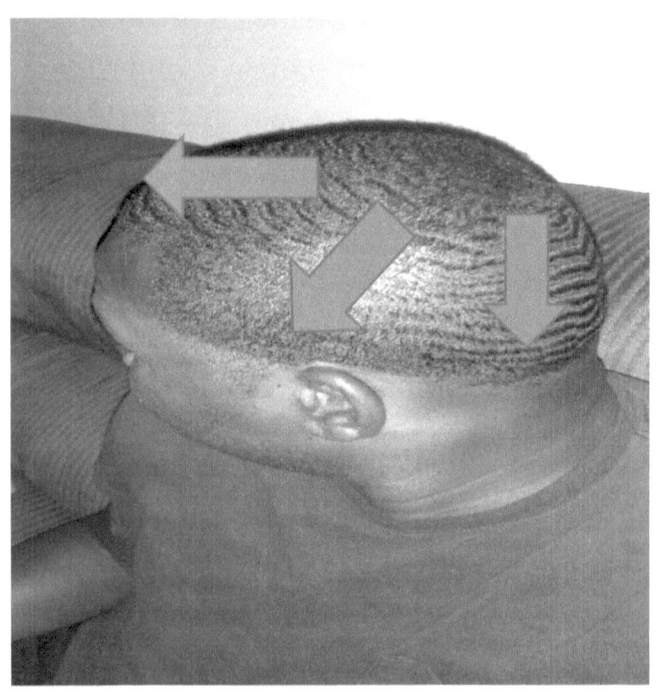

The Right Brush

The curve brush is the most popular brush on the market these days and why because it hits every corner of the hair, and a good medium brush will give you the right pull and help you through a strong two day brush session. You will need to brush two hours a day and that will be a hour in the morning and a hour at night and why because nappy hair needs to be train to go in the right direction, because those nappy strings believe it or not turns into waves it will take three weeks depending on how you brush and it will turn into wavy hair, and some people get a table fade and focus on the top and brush strong to get them waves, and some people are born with wavy natural hair.

But to put together three layers on both sides and the back of the hair will give you that popular look, but nothing cannot be accomplish if you do not put the time are effort in your brush session, and you should stay away from them supper hard brushes because a good strong medium will do with natural boar bristles, and brushing in a pattern is very important and ladies compliment men with good hair.

The Right Hair Grease

Murrys pomade is the right hair grease to get your waves started and to get your hair train so that you can start seeing good progress, you will not have to use a lot of hair grease because murrys pomade is very thick grease and you should use it right meaning not to much, because if you put to much it could bring your edges out and that is when it is very thick to your hair. Murrys pomade lays the hair down and when applying a good durag it can show awesome change to your waves because it is all about taking care of your hair,.But it is not the same, and remember Murrys pomade is a classic when it comes to taking care of your hair. Murrys pomade is for great hair growth and great training for expert wavers and some beginners, and this will be one major way that each wave in your hair will connect, and once your waves connect try a can of murrys pomade light and it will also become a perfect grease to use, and give quality shine to your hair not quantity.

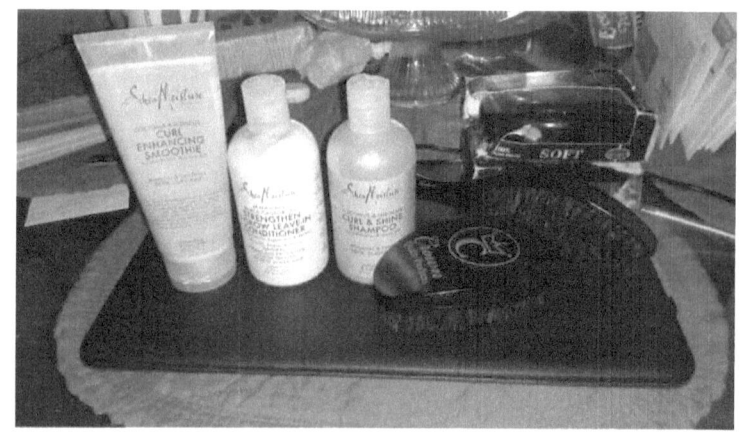

Brushing Method

The down ward angle brushing toward your chin on the sides and applying the straight downward angle on the back and brushing forward on the top. You the 360 waver will repeat this method as much as you can and you will not need to count the stroke of the brush, or always talking while the camera is on, but you will have to brush by the minute and brush until you hit that hour brush session, and don't think because you don't see the progress of your hustle by brushing your hair, but understand this it will not form into the 360 wave position in a week, but as you keep your brush session going toward the second week then you see the nappy hair that we are bless with form into waves or wavy hair.

And by you continuing on with the brush session toward week 3, and wearing your durag right before bed and then you will see some major results of seeing some 360 waves form into a ocean, the fourth week is one month and continuing on with a strong brush session and following the method you have chosen then you will begin to go through the next step and now your waves should be stable by you staying committed to your method and brush session.

The Right Durag

Why shop for a fancy durag and why haven't you notice that the durag is one of the most important methods for keeping your 360 waves in place, now when your through with each brush session you will need to use a little of murrys light pomade, and then lay your durag on the hair properly, so that your 360 waves will begin to join together in the way you brush them to. And you should learn to sleep with your durag on every night, and keep it in a place where you can found it and also keep your durag clean much as possible so that you can use it again. Okay listen to this even the dollar store sell silk wave durags and stocking caps, so that your hair will be able to continue to grow properly, and have that unique 360 wave look, so sleep with your durag on and wake up with your durag on.

Shower Method

HOW TO GET 360 WAVES

Okay lets get to it as a beginner waver you do not need to wash your hair every day, but the method is to wash your hair once a week, because if you wash your hair every day as a beginner or even a pro waver it can effect your waves. Squave shampoo is good and when you shower make sure you have your brush, and while the water is running just commit to start brushing toward the chin on each side and in a downward position on the back side, and brush forward on the top and when its time to dry your hair, and then add some blue magic hair grease, because this will start another method and help your hair grow to be healthty and continue to grow.

Because as you keep brushing the stronger the connection will be and when its time to get and hair cut you will be amaze how fare you have come as a 360 waver has come, and be careful with the shae moisturizer because you don't want your hair to be to soft okay.

Mosturizer

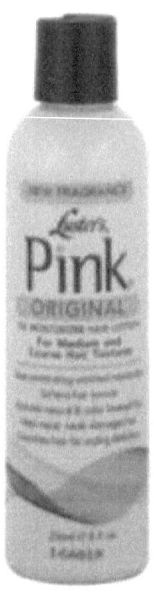

Blue magic coconut oil is the prime suspect for getting 360 waves, because as wavers, this is use when it is time to dress your hair after a long one hour or and thirty minute brush session. The ingredient gives and awesome shine to your hair to make the hair soft, this conditioner helps the hair to grow and it gives the hair a more shinny look, and it do not break the edges off of your hair and it is very able to keep the waves in place after your durag is remove.

When your applying this conditioner try to keep it away from the four head, and that include all types of 360 waves accessories because the skin is very sensitive. This can also be applied by using murrys pomade and with a little shea moisturizer and then apply a durag over your hair.

360 Wave Style Pomade

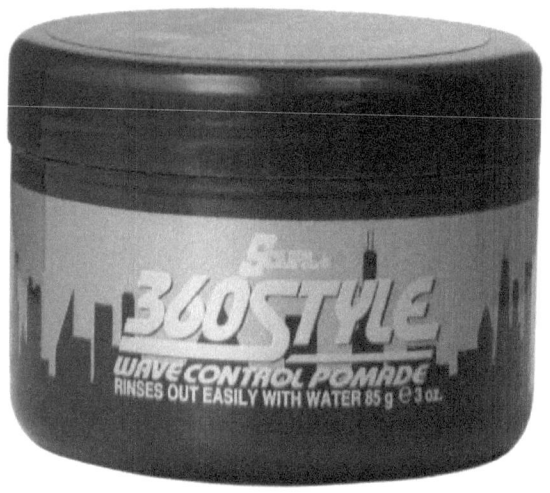

This product is for beginners it gives a soft touch to the hair and also and exclusive shine to the hair as well, and the look is awesome and way more quality then you think the brush session is and keeping your hair up is the method and applying the durag after a hard working brush session. Why do we use these types of products as 360 wavers because murrys pomade is to thick and when applying it sticks to the hand as well, it is thick when applying on the hair, now this product is a lite pomade and it has a very lite layer and it gives your waves a sporty look just as well as a professional look.

And when it is applied and afterward apply your durag, and leave it on for a couple of hours and when you remove the durag the hair is ready for the public and your waves are very noticeable to the eye, and this is a great tip to share or show other wavers on your Facebook fan page or Youtube Page But try not to use it every day but it can be applied twice a week, and a little of hair grease.

YouTube 360 Wavers

HOW TO GET 360 WAVES

As a 360 waver we cannot get caught up in social media and seeing those famous wavers can make you want to be in front of them \ camera all day, with their awesome waves and we cannot hate on the next 360 waver in this wave game, Because they have a big following and that is known as subscribers. You have to focus on your method and keeping your 360 waves in the best shape as possible, you must remember your waves is not going to look like those wavers, and those wavers hair is not going to look like yours, because the subscribers is going to come as long as you do not try to act like another waver.

Because there are wavers that have been

waveing for over twenty years and some 360 wavers have over 300,000 subscribers and that is a fan base. You are the teacher to the next waver because if you choose to start your own 360 wave page ,questions are going to be ask , and people will need TIPS, so always answer your followers back on time.

Stay Away From Relaxers

When you're a 360 waver you are after trying to keep all strings on your hair down and you are not satisfied with your natural hair as it look, the relaxer will lay the front and sides down as well as the back of your hair. And when you use a relaxer kit your hair become very soft and it will look good, but it will not stand up to a hard brush are in a hour brush session, and even with a medium brush your waves will soon fade away, because of the strong chemicals the relaxer carry inside the kit.

Now it will all come down to you as the 360 waver to just be yourself because there are more people who appreciate a natural look then a dishonest look, because the hair is a part of our everyday dress code and our hair represent the way we look at home , work, in public, and when we are out with the wife, that's why I choose to support 360 waves and much respect to the guys with waves, on top of their game supporting 360 waves. Because I love to give advice about 360 waves

Shae Moisturizer

And it can also make your waves disconnect
for the moment and go all over the place.
But the look it gives is curls and a powerful
shinnie look and the 360 waves will still look
strong to the public. Some wavers do not
understand waves because waves can be
brush into curls and they also can be brush
back into waves, Because that is what shae
moisturizer is made for to give the
customers that use it that soft groovie
natural look, shae moisture also make the
hair grow and that's why you should only
use it once a week, the medium brush is the
best brush to use in the brush session when
this product is applied, because the hard
brush can pull soft hair out of it's possession.

But I would strongly recommend you use it because the hair still do need to grow, for the waves to connect and come together as one.

The Wolfing Method

Do you want to see powerful waves and do you the 360 waver want to see a ocean as they lay still on your head, the tip of the day will be washing and conditioning and growing your hair out foor a couple of months, and when it's time to see your results and in time your hair will form well and when your wolfing trial is over it is time to head to the barber. But only if you can get the one or two guard to cut over your hair, because if so your waves will put a small on your face because the 360 wave method of waveing has payed off, and you the 360 waver need to learn how to cut your own hair , because I truely believe when the barber cuts his on hair the better the results, wolfing is a factor in the wave game to make your waves strong and perfect and the quality from your wolfing will speak for it self.

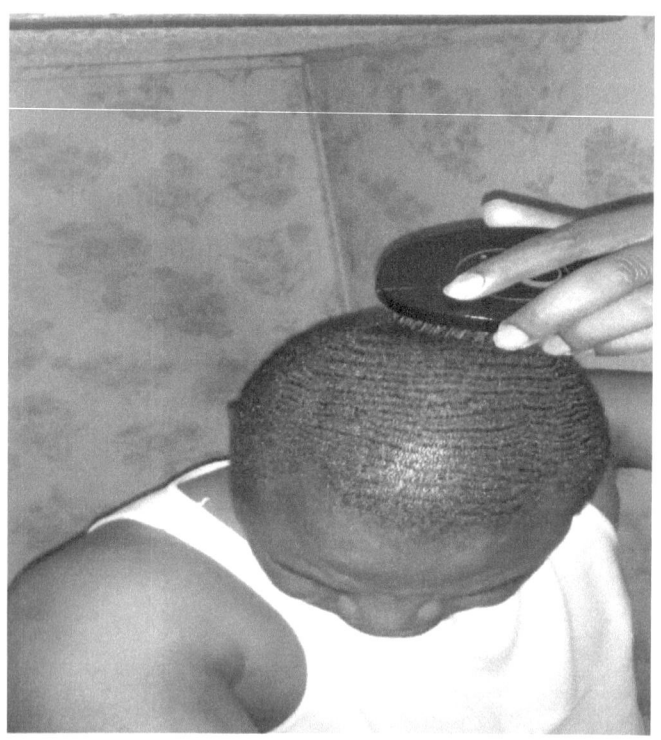

The Right Clippers To Cut 360 waves

When you are using your on clippers in the

HOW TO GET 360 WAVES

wave game and cutting your own hair it can take you to high places in the 360 wave industry.

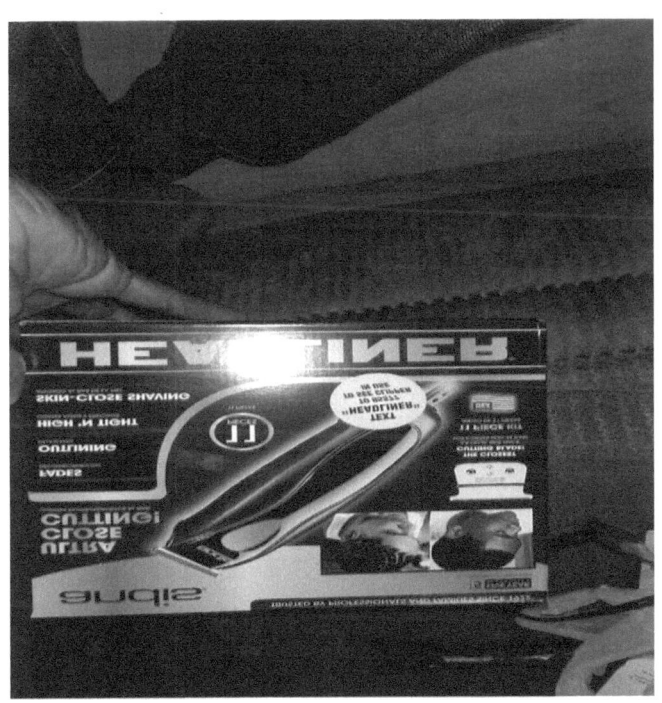

HOW TO GET 360 WAVES

Annie are some of the most powerful clippers to use in the wave game right now today because when you the waver cut your own hair live on YOUTUBE, it show the subscribers that you are a force to be wrecken with. You see many people or should I say barbers cannot cut waves or natural hair and when you're the 360 waver and the barber well, how bout you focus on cutting your on hair and other **360 WAVERS HAIR also.**

And make the effort to show the beginners the way to cut hair and use Annie adjustable clippers or the classic brand call wahles clippers. Because these clippers put your waves and the customer hair against the graind, you see the right clippers blades or not spreaded out but are perfectly fit to make the hair cut and hair lines and edge up come out perfectly, and your 360 waves will be perfectly as ever.

Tips Is Very Powerful

When I fir st started waveing I needed help so I turn to youtube to see what the teachers of the wave game had to offer. I wanted my waves to be notice by any one who saw me out in public, , because when I first started off no one seem to notice because they did not feel the same about their hair like I did. But what I learn from experience wavers is the game, about what 360 waves meant in the urban community. And that was the history of waveing and how you can have great hair as a black men.

HOW TO GET 360 WAVES

And that could lead to good texture, and to grind for nice waves that can make the next waver up set. The tips of learning to use murrys pomade and how to brush correctly and how to use hot oil treatments and to make my 360 waves look the best, I learned about the right brush to use and the brushes not to use. I learn how to respect the game, and how you can build your own brand by selling brushes, and learning many methods as I can and showing your hair in hair shows, and learning many methods as I can for healthy hair and for healthy hair and for healthy 360 waves that will help the next person or kid to have strong hair, because on my fan page I give tips all the time, so me as a waver I have to provide tips to them my

33

followers.

Vaseline

Yes you can get 360 waves from using Vaseline and you can because your brushing method will stay the same. You will have a more or should I say a natural look and your waves will be in demand and visible to the eye of the people that is around you, my brother Terry Huffman was in the justice system once upon a time, and when I went to visit him his hair was the best and I said to him what you use on your hair, and he said Vaseline, and he said I brush all day because there is nothing else to do. And his hair was straith and his hair was not greasy but it was very shinnie and healthy, and his method gave 360 waves a great look because he put in the time and effort.

And using whatever he could to make his waves and hair to be powerful looking, and the method on his hair stood out. So I encourage you to make use of what you got that will give your 360 waves the best result that you can.

Dax Pomade

his pomade is hype and really the only different is, it is more of a grease pomade and it can make your hair shiny are it can make your hair thin for the moment, are when it dry it can become very hard then dry, but it is still a good product to have and I did a video on Dax pomade, and I feel it is for the wavers to choose and to try a 360 wave product on there on. I guess what I'm trying to get at is, don't go broke behind wave products or should I say hair products that other wavers use, it all come down to the method that you create and use, when

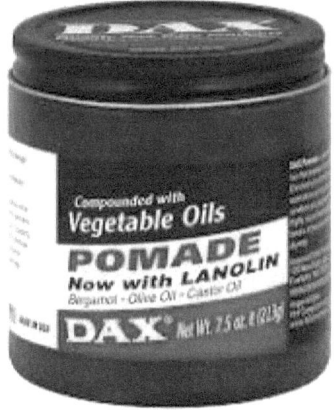

you use

a product don't over do it.

And when you make a 360 wave video on Dax pomade like me give the subscribers the best report because it is up to you to research the product before you use it, so why let your hair fall out on a 360 wave none product that you do not have a clue about. But before I end this paragraph I give Dax pomade 3 stars.

Do Expensive Brushes Get You 360 Waves

Yes depending on the brush and how you brush because you cannot be getting broke behind 360 waves or any type of hair style, but the curve brush is one of the most powerful brushes and why because how the brush curve and how it fits the sides of your head. But you still have to use products with any brush you buy no matter how expensive or cheap the brush is, because it is about the brush session and the time you put in using this brush, because you still have to use grease and apply a durag, and with any price of a brush you still have to have patients.

Building Subscribers In The 360 Wave Game

The only way you can build a strong audience in the 360 wave game is by being try to what you do and how you carry yourself, in front of the camera because most fans or subscribers expect you to answer back if the message are tip is ask for. You as the 360 waver have to reach back and give back to your followers by chateng with them, you see subscribers love feed back exspecally when they see that you are being treated with the best In the 360 wave game.

Okay all things don't last forever but good hair can and by you spreading the good 360 wave news about how to get 360 waves, because your 360 waves followers love when you are being the teacher. Fans like it when they can hear you explain about the product, and the steps it will take to maintain and get the look they need to get quality 360 waves and why they subscribe to your channel in the first place, because they love the feedback.

360 Waves Battles And Beefs

HOW TO GET 360 WAVES

I once did a video call behind the 360 waves process scam and the reason I did that video because I was new to the game. And the reason I did the video because I was new to the game. I mean I got a lot of hate mail and also a lot of keeping it real mail, because a lot of 360 wavers was talking about my rough hair and they didn't feel me, because I did not use the relaxer or perm , all I use was grease and so I got upset and came at all the experience wavers and believe it or not I was wrong and it didn't give me a lot of followers.

But I still had to get my point a cross because some of the big dogs was commenting on the video. But I did the dumbest thing I took the video down because what was done was done, but I had to start growing in the wave game and I would not beef again.

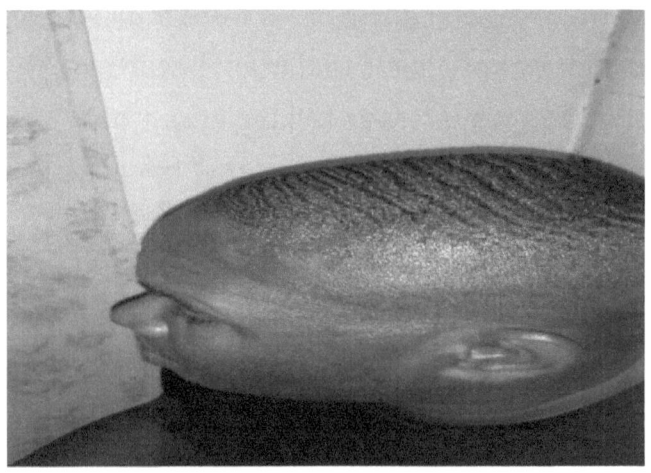

But these brothers have some very awesome waves and yes it be a lot of beef and jealousy in the 360 wave game, and especially when your being sponsored and getting paid to promote up coming wave brushes or other company brushes, and getting first dips on new 360 waves accessories and doing qualities videos, and cutting top wavers hair in the 360 wave game, so yes they beef and I have battle in the 360 wave game.

Chapter 2

The 360 Waves Process Continue

As a 360 waver you cannot distance yourself away from your family, because I have watch a lot of videos when the kids come knocking on the rest room door and dad gets mad because he is doing a video session, okay listen it is alright to love what you do but to distinct yourself away from your family is a selfish act, because as a waver you have to understand that we will onde day get old, and 50% of us the 360 wavers will lose our hair, but by being a 360 waver we shouldn't let stress or worrying take our hair away from its roots, but family and kids or a bound so do not stop your children from coming in to support your brush session are talk to you, put your children in your brush session. And they may come in the brush session causing war.

ell dad give them a brush and train them your sons how to get 360 waves. Because it is good to have wavy hair and to have over 100,00 thousand subscribers, but it is not worth destroying your relationship with your family.

The Stocking Cap Method

This is a great day and time in my hood for all wavers and 360 wavers, you must treat your waves or your hair to become very a live or shiny, this day time method is call the stocking cap method but the material is stronger than using a woman stocking for a wave cap, the stocking cap helps the hair breed and it keeps the waves packed down in other words train your hair to lay down, you see the stocking cap should not be taking for granted in the 360 wave game, because the stocking cap isn't just a method but a solution to training your 360 waves.

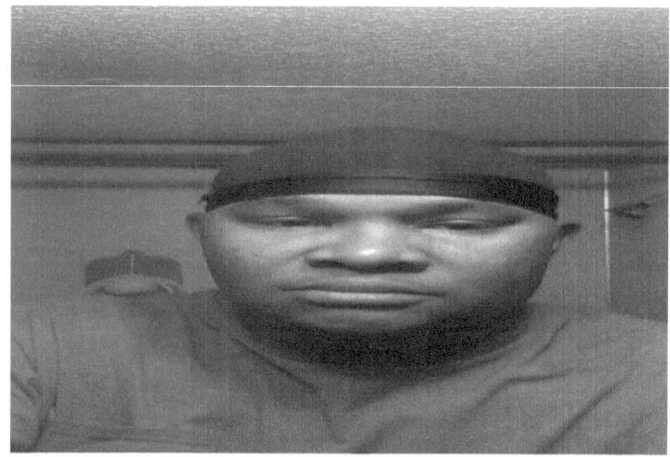

Curly hair it once was you who had nappy hair and as you brush and applied the product that is needed, then you can use the stocking cap over your durag and will give the right pressure fit over your hair, so that the products that are applied can marinate threw the hair and scape, and when the stocking cap is

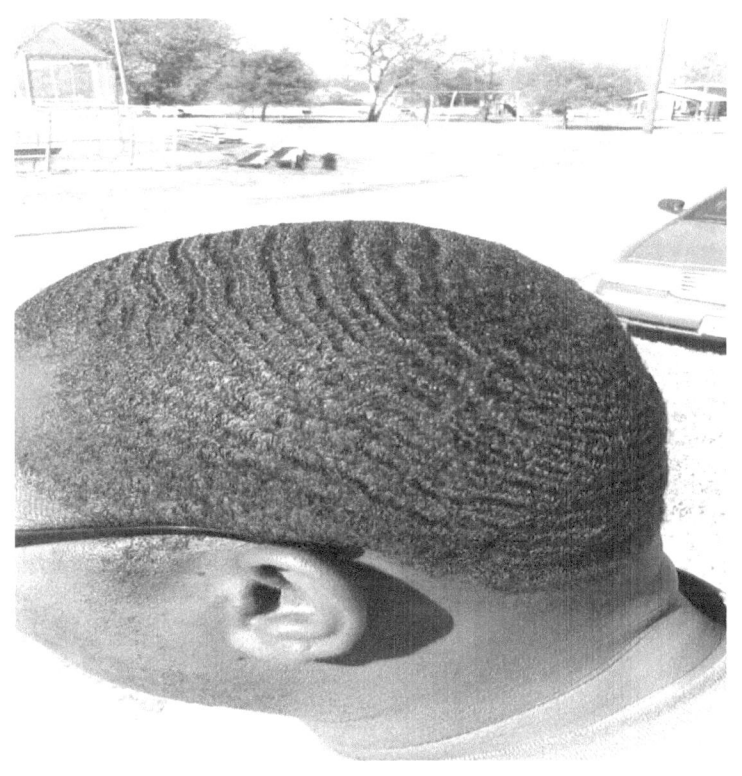

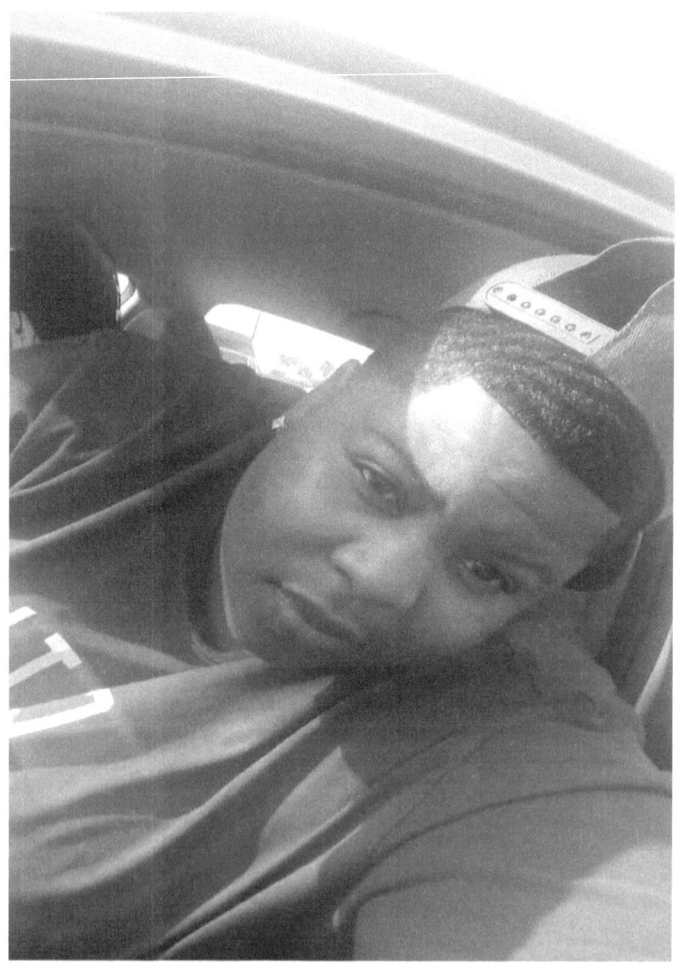

HOW TO GET 360 WAVES

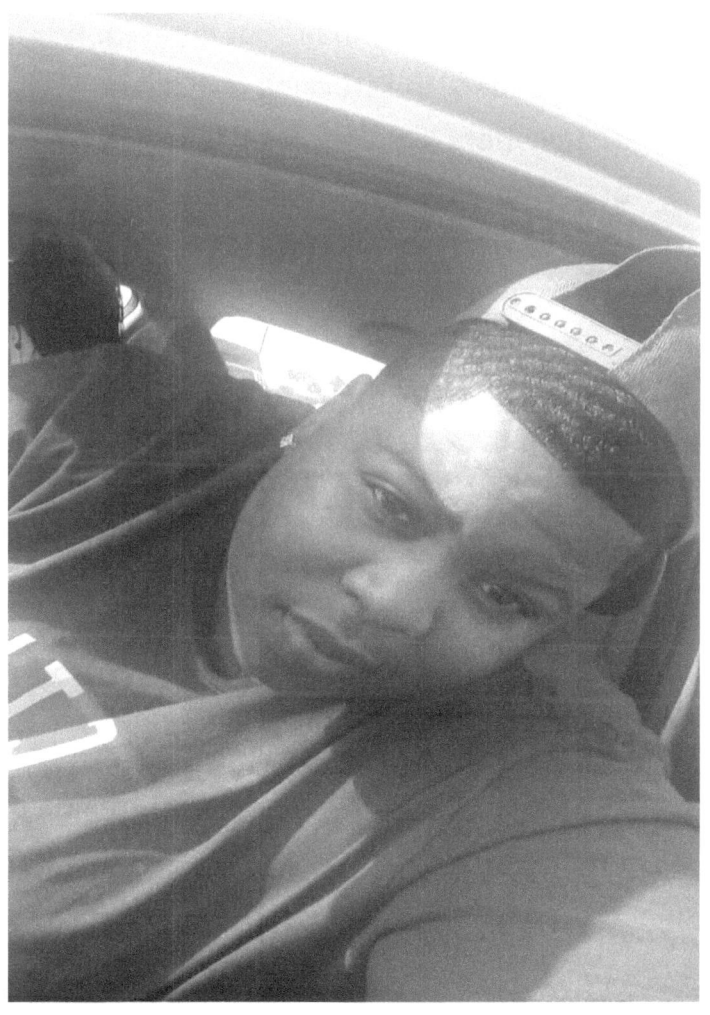

remove this give your hair that great look that's needed, the stocking cap can be bought anywhere like your local family dollar stores, and once applied it will get you started as a 360 waver.

Can Women Get Wavse

Yes they can get 360 waves are waves with a table fade and the look can be sporty just like the men, 360 waves are for different genders are should I say male and female, it is not hard but you as the 360 waver have to start putting the time in threw out each brush session, so with this being said check out my cousin 360 waves style girl picture.

HOW TO GET 360 WAVES

So when you feel it is not easy to get 360 waves brush and for some people when they cut they hair you never know what type of texture is under the layer of your hair, so can women get 360 waves yes and can they look just as good as the men yes they can, so stay focus and 360 waves out.

Murrys Bees Wax Grease

This grease can be damaging to the hair and it could give the hair the right sporty look if use right, but if you apply to much it could damage your hair and when the brush is applied it could leave a spot in your head meaning ball spot in your head. Yes it is a pomade it can have your waves looking good and it can have your waves laid down to the tee and be hitting at all corners, but as a waver we cannot be depending on one product because the tip has to be given about the product and you as the 360 waver should share how this grease is use, and how much is needed to be use or applied, murrys bees wax is not expensive and you can also find this product on your shelves at your local family dollar for a good price. And you can also find many more hair products.

Hot Oil Treatments

Step 1. You will need to set the hot oil treatment in a warm bowl of hot water until it is ready to apply to your hair, and you can also use the hot oil product cold on your 360 waves, apply the oil and let it soften the hair for 30 minutes before brushing, then after 30 minutes you should commits to brushing it in and also after you brush for 20 minutes or 30 minutes, apply durag and let the durag stay on all night are for two hours, and when you remove the durag you will see the method and treatment that the hot oil product has done for your hair.

HOW TO GET 360 WAVES

You see the hot oil is fertilize for your hair and scalp so that your hair can be wavy and black and soft, and it can be come a natural look and it makes the hair look just right for the next upcoming wave journey for you to take your hair to the next level, just remember these products can harm your eyes if not use or clean probably, and there is other hot oil products which is the growth oil and it is also and hot oil that can help your hair, and hot oil conditioners can help your hair, and also including the subject of this book which is how to get 360 waves.

For each product to give you the right 360 waves and there is and solution with each product bought.

Stay A Way From S curl Gel

As a black men you should never be a shame of your hair because the thicker the hair the stronger the results, okay your waves may look good but for some reason you as the 360 waver is very please with these results, but you wonder why your hair do not look like this waver hair. But the way you lay it is out, the tips of how you got your waves but just be you and do not apply s curl gel to your hair because it is soft one minute and hard the next minute.

And after you apply s curl gel the first time and your happy because of the look it gave your hair, but it will make your hair look a mess the next time when you use it, and if you ignore this tip and you choose to use this product it can change are damage you're your waves into a terrible look, and if you put a kit in, you will give up a strong brush session, because straigth hair is not always the best hair for 360 waves, but always keep brushing to improve your hair for strong waves.

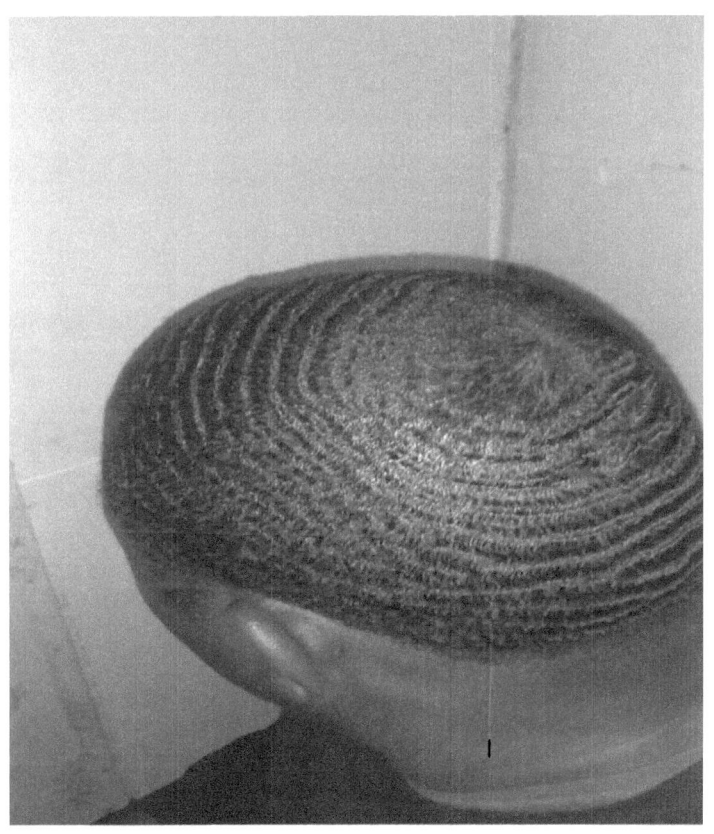

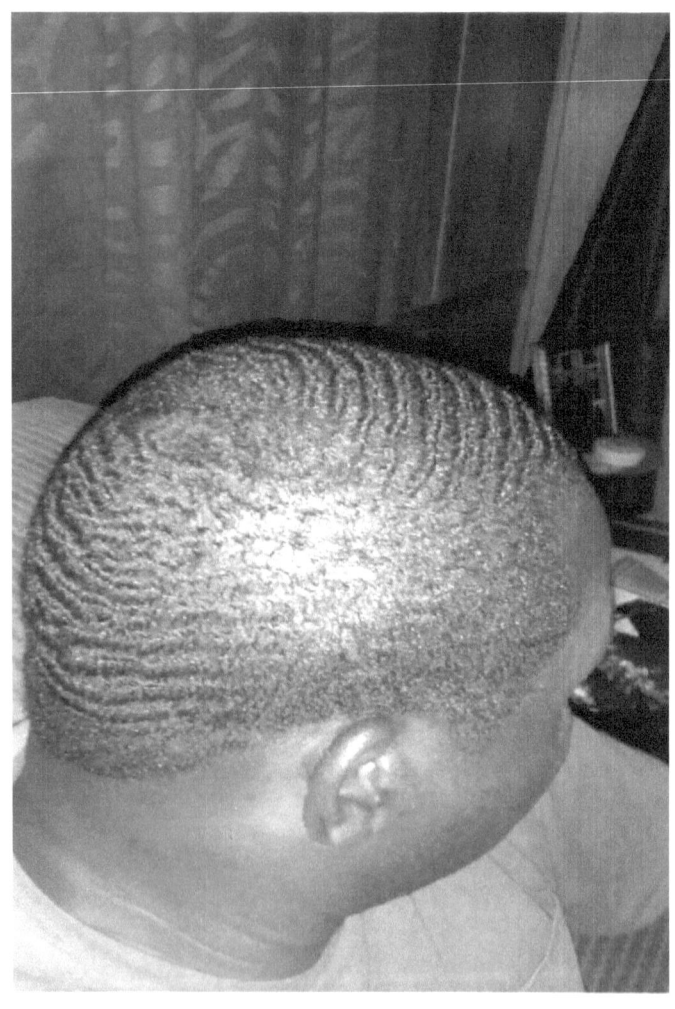

360 Wave Golden

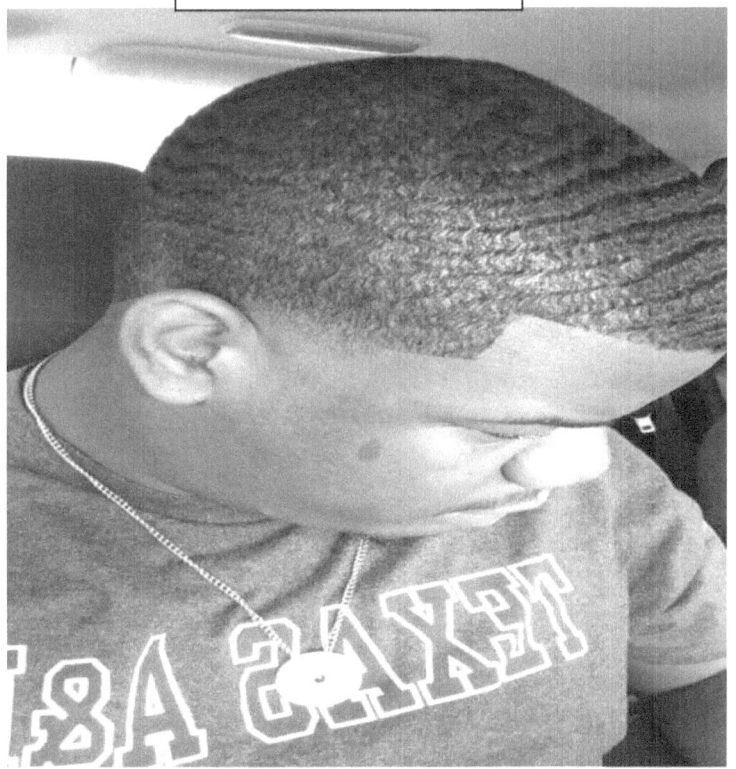

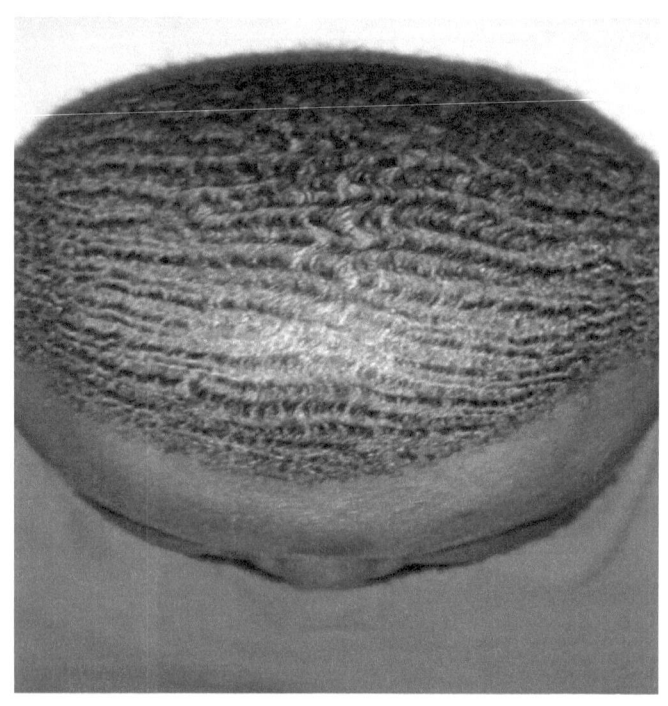

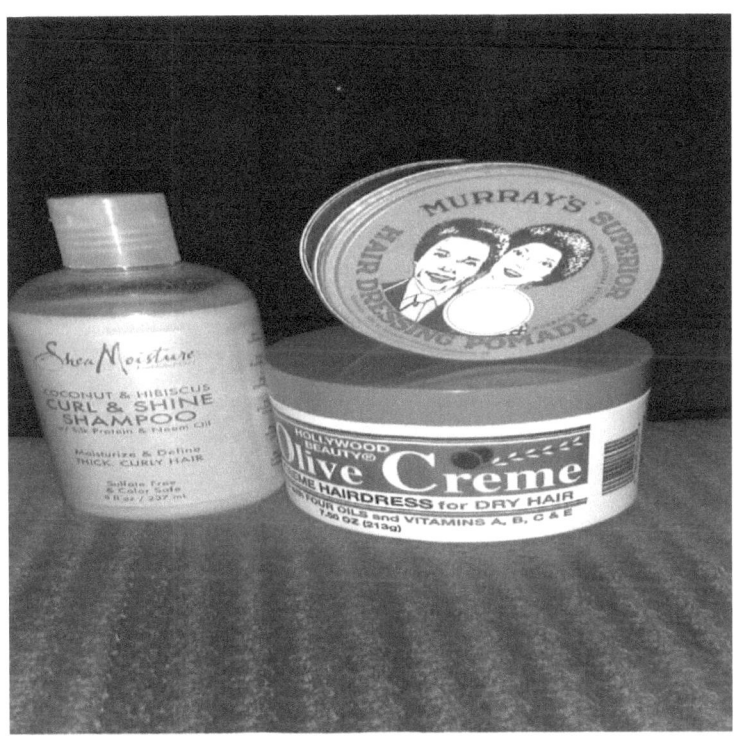

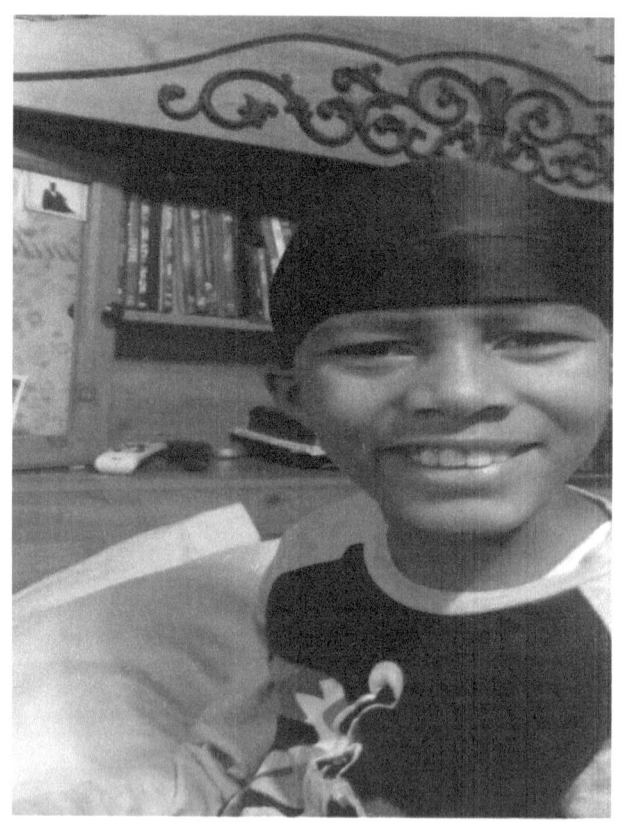

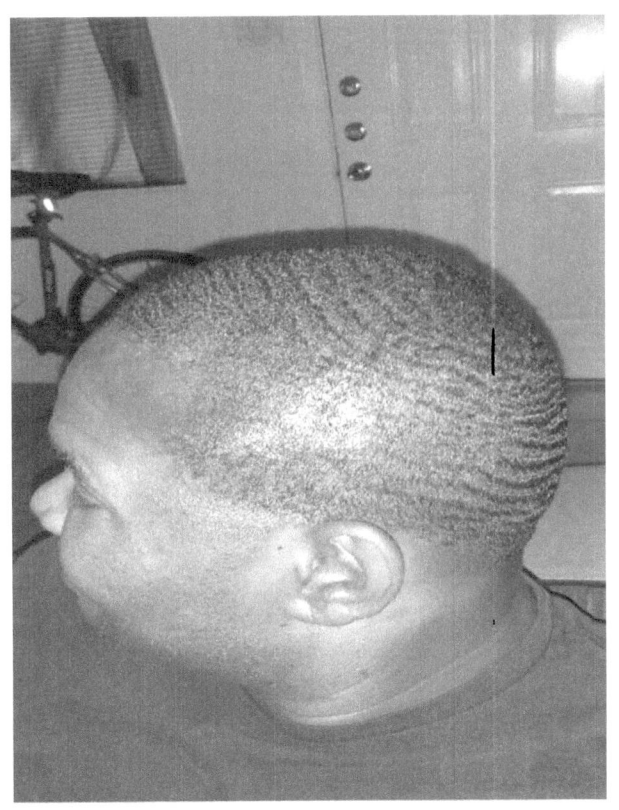

HOW TO GET 360 WAVES

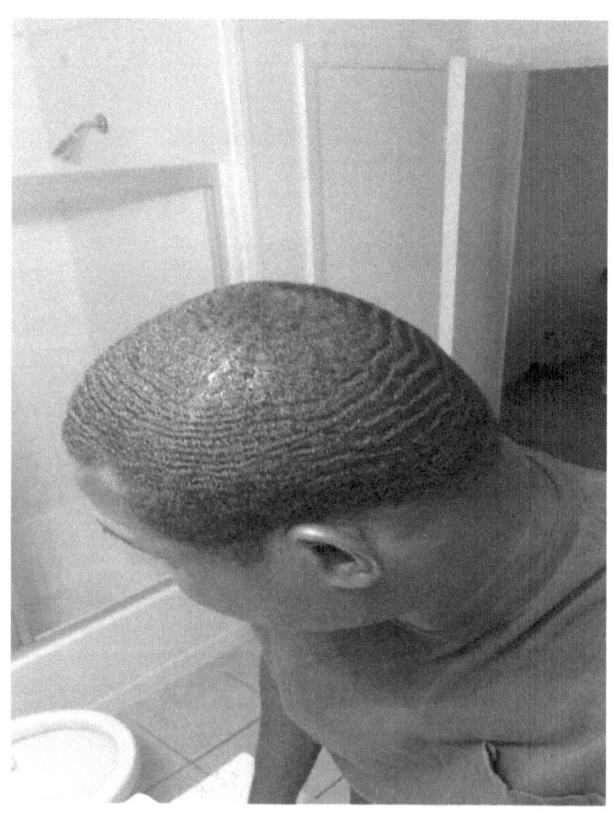

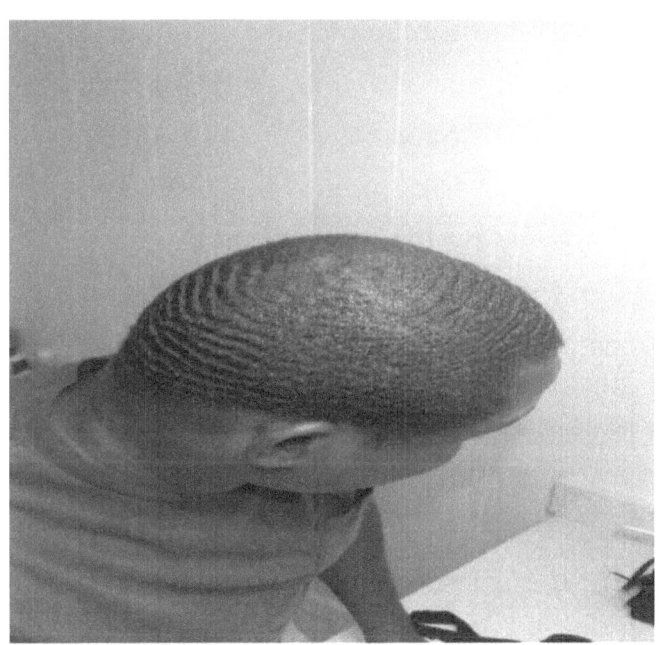

The Weak Side

When you are able to get waves on the right side of your hair and not on the left, that becomes the weak side, because you not brushing enough on one side of your hair, I suggest you to do a and extra hour on your weak side to catch it up with the strong side of your hair because all it takes is time and more effort to complete the 360 wave circle that you are looking for, so I suggest you to go for it and get them waves and rock them waves.

Conclusion

The art of getting 360 wavse is a book for the black culture and all cultures with rough hair, because 360 waves is a part of your every day look and dress code, you should love the way your hair look and you should want to share tips about how to get them 360 waves so keep waving and God bless, and this book is written by yours truly 360 Waves Deep Pizza.

HOW TO GET 360 WAVES

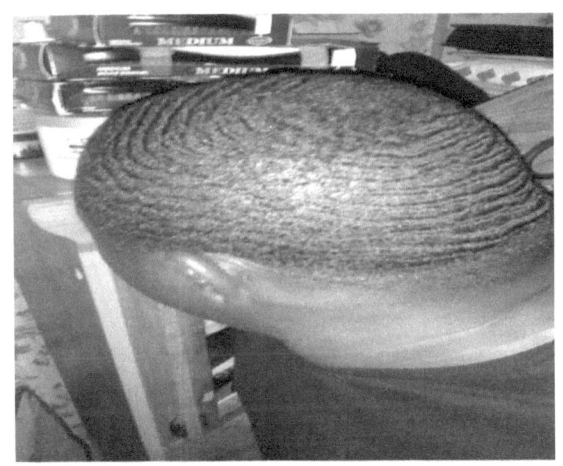

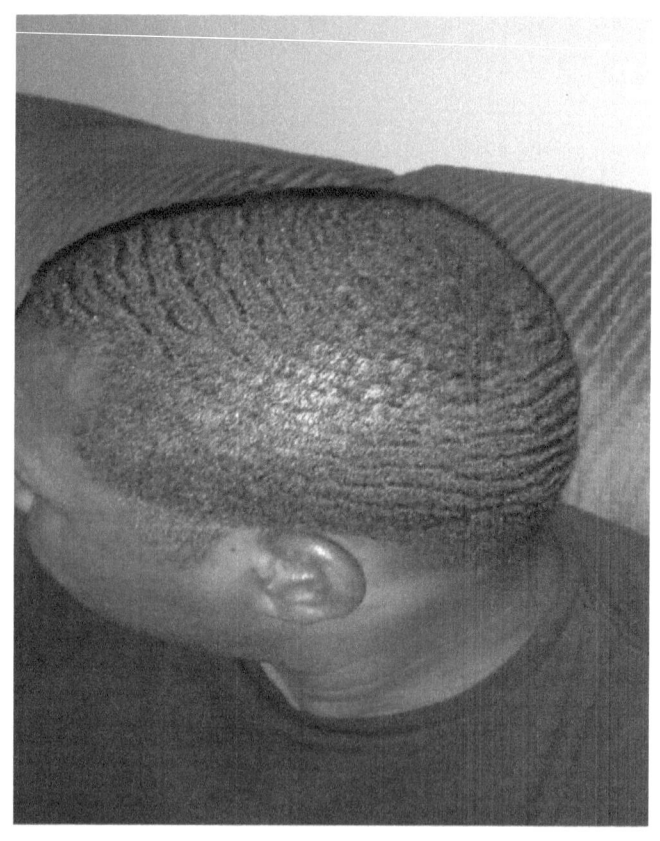

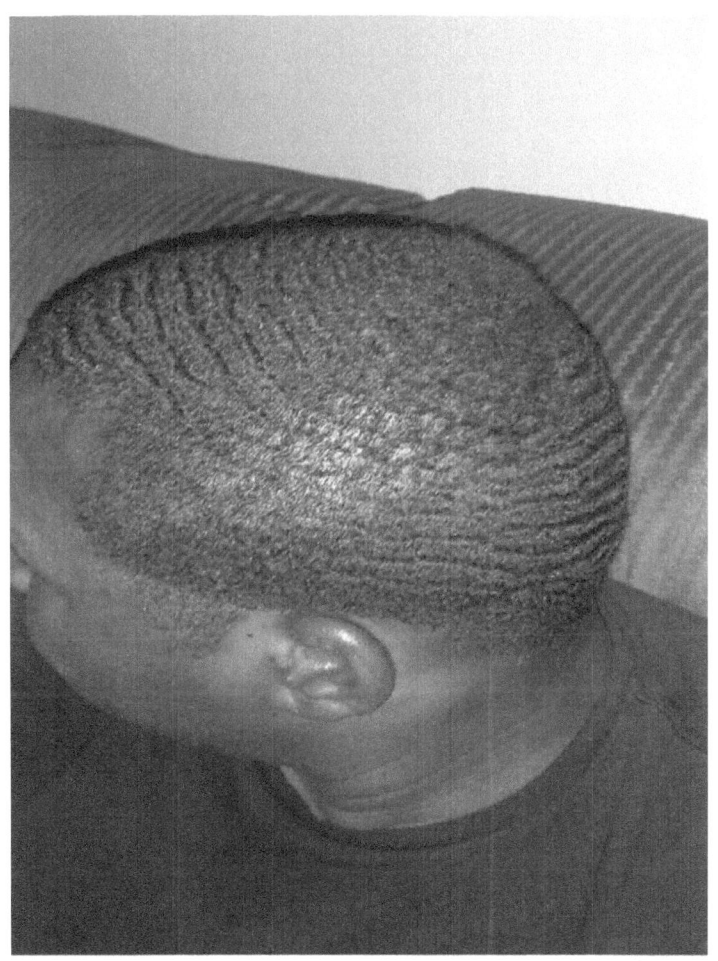

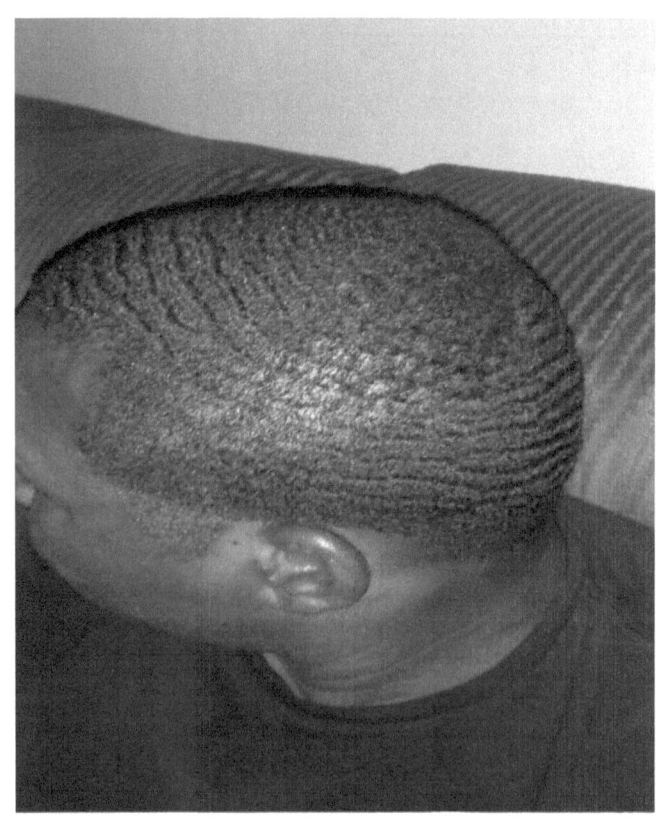

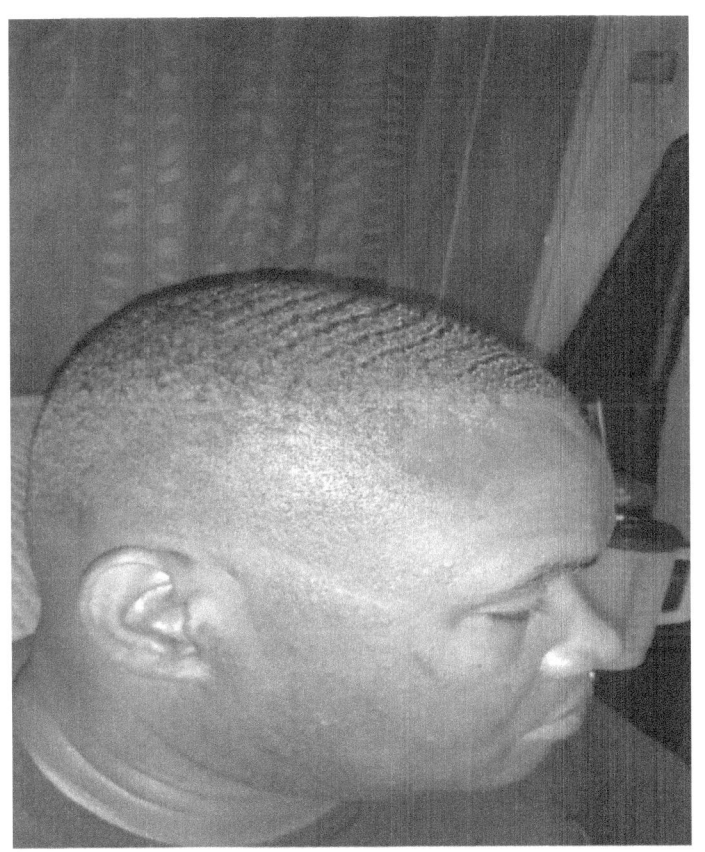

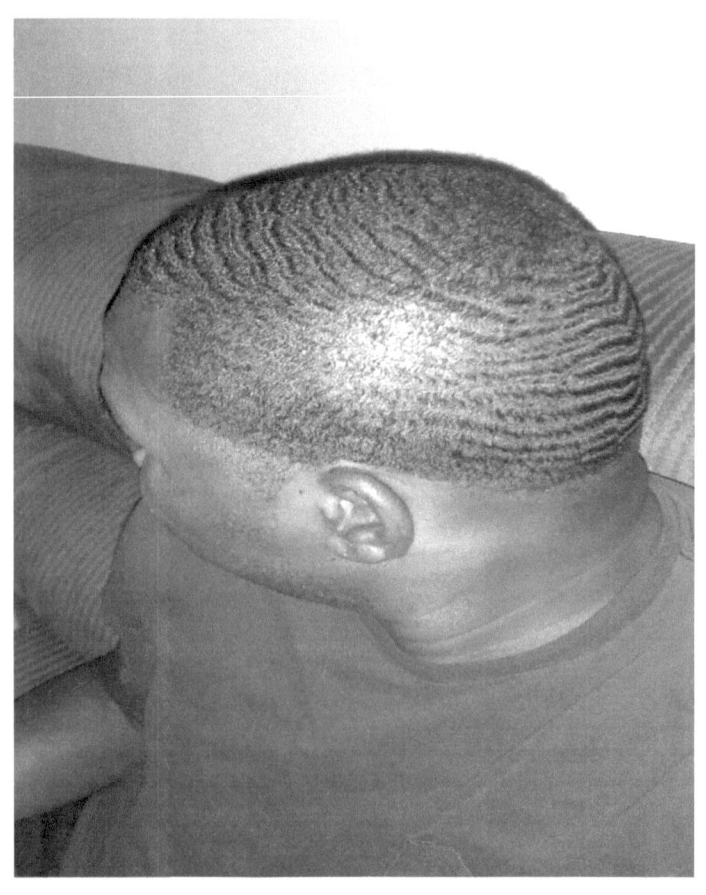

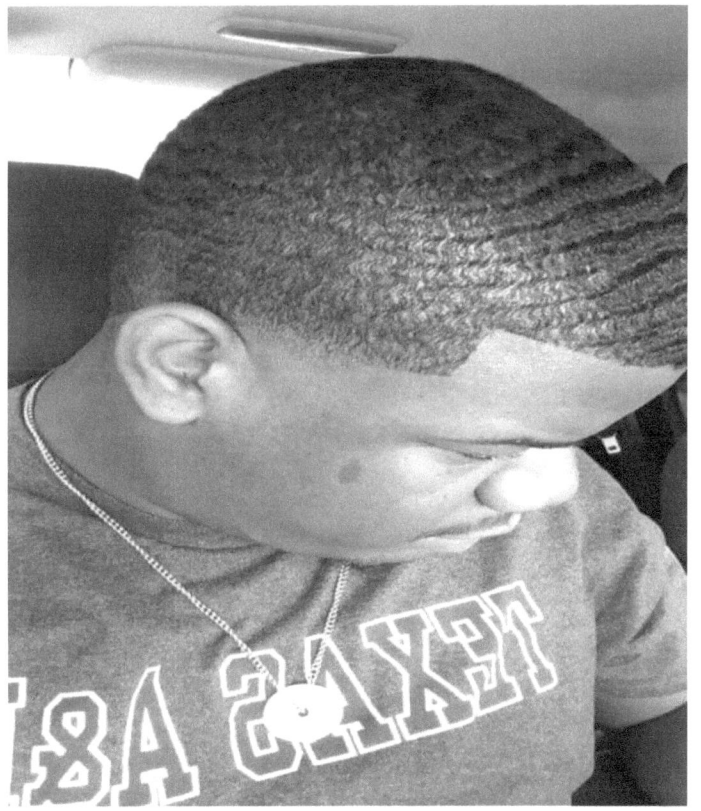

360 Wave Golden

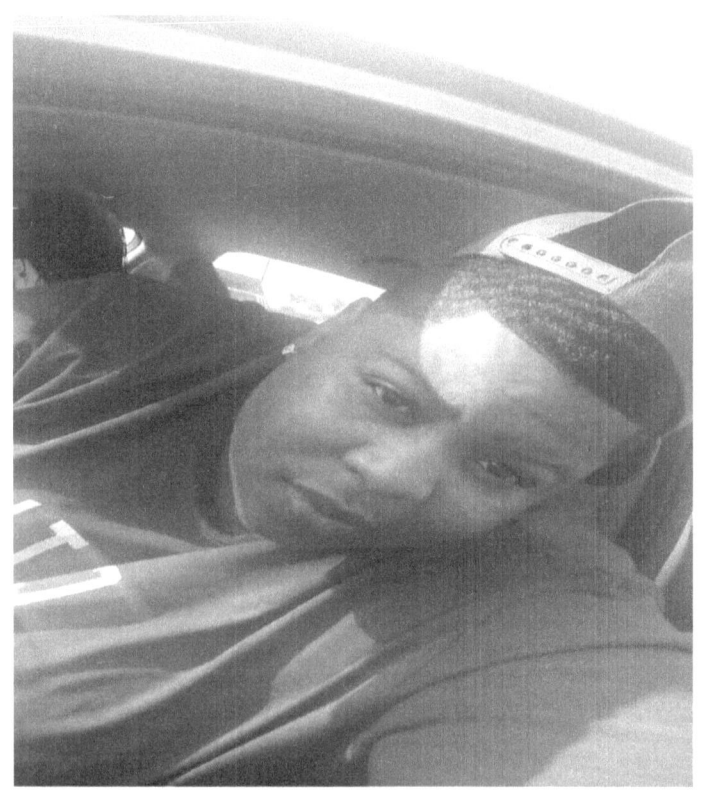

360 Wave style girl

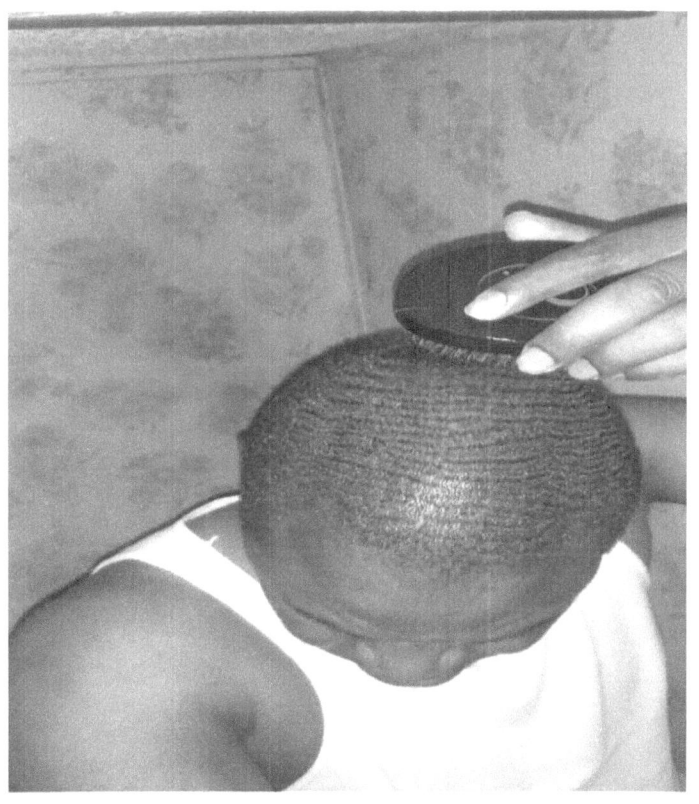

CQP Show the waves approve

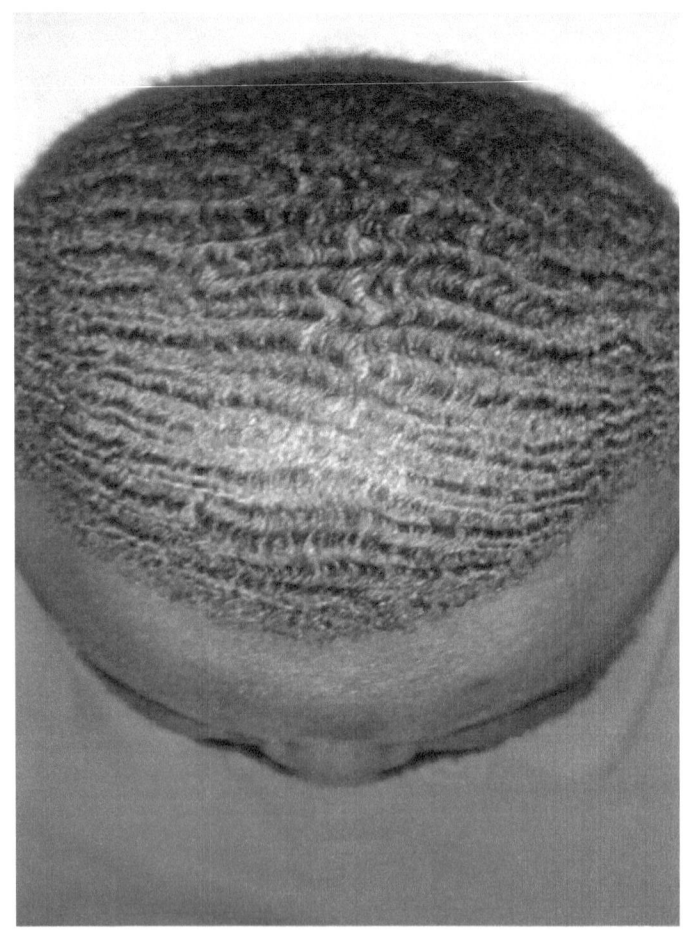

360 wave fan page follower shonn

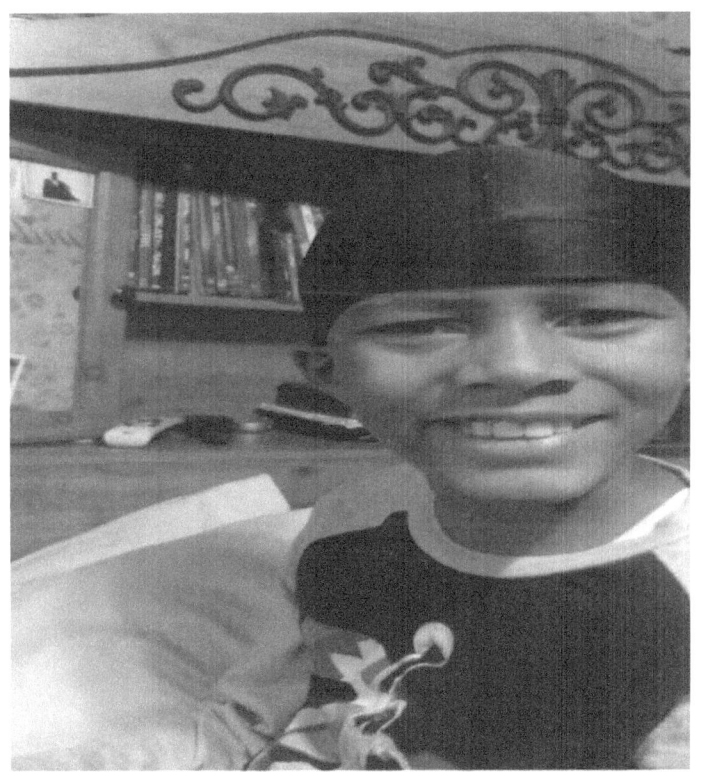

#60 Wavers Isaac, and TJ

HOW TO GET 360 WAVES

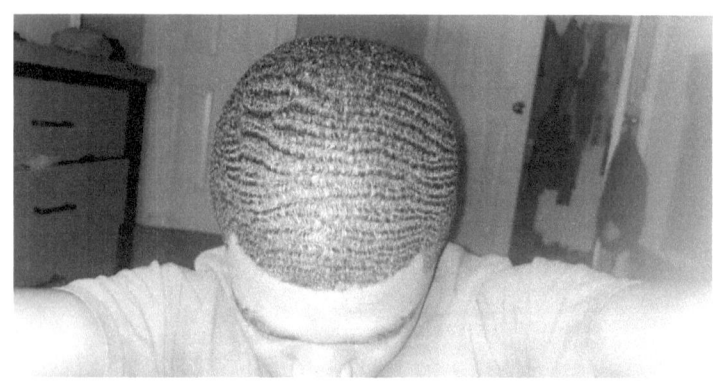

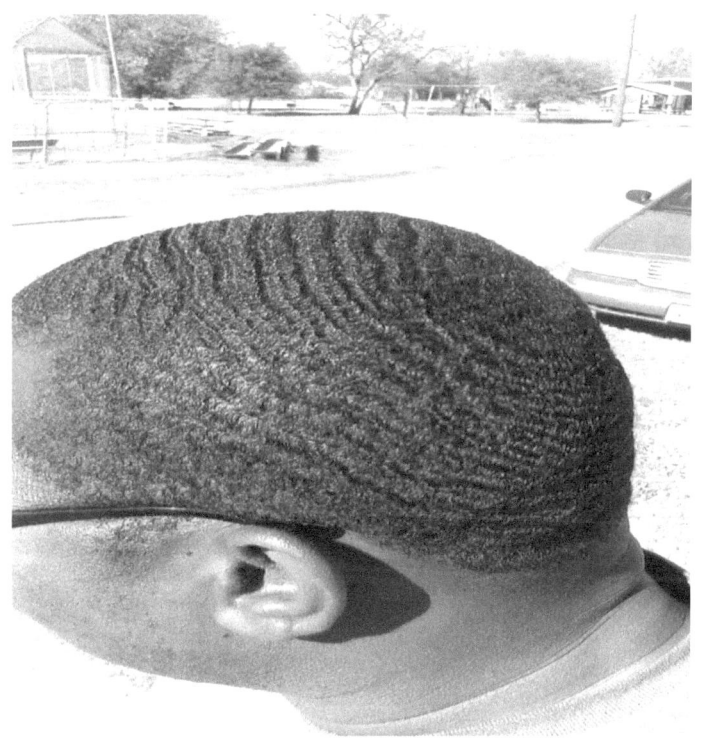

Let the sun hit the ocean

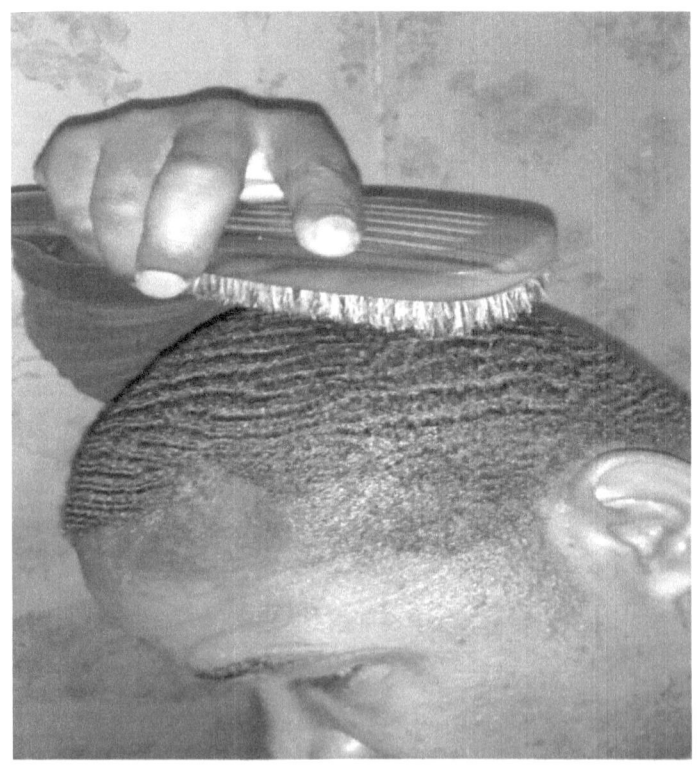

Brushing gets you waves

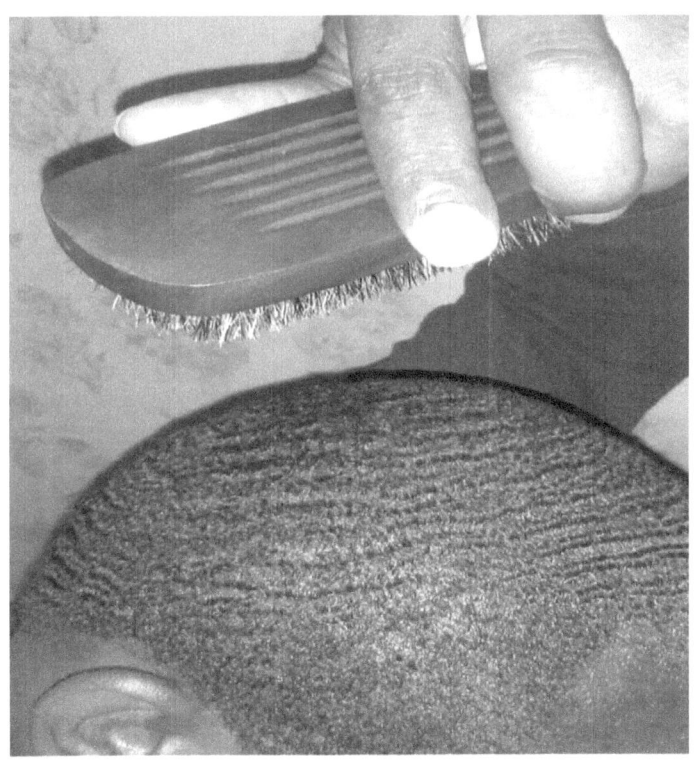

Brushing Method gets waves

Weak side of my hair but still as a waver you

Have to brush smarter.

Brush hard and don't cheap the brush sessions bless the brush session

SHOW REULTS AND GIVE TIPS.

Special Thanks

360 Wave Golden, 360 Wave T J, #360 Wave Style Girl,

360 Wave Isaac, And to all my followers on
my fanpage.

360 Waves

Forever

360 Waves

Forever

360 Waves

Forever

360 Waves Forever

360 Waves Forever

360 Waves

Forever

360 Waves

Forever

360 Waves

Forever

360 Waves

Forever